Shadows of
St Andrews Past

SHADOWS of St ANDREWS PAST

DAVID · W · LYLE

JOHN DONALD PUBLISHERS LTD
EDINBURGH

This book is lovingly dedicated to my best friend and wife: Carol

ISBN 0 85976 280 7

Typeset by Newtext Composition Ltd., Glasgow
Printed in Great Britain by Bell & Bain Ltd., Glasgow

Acknowledgements

I AM GRATEFUL to many local people who gave freely of their old books, pamphlets and photographs, but above all I acknowledge my debt to those who shared their personal memories. They told many unrecorded facts about the community life of St Andrews past which predate my own experience, each story being an invaluable contribution to the creation of this book.

There is another group of select individuals who have given me the benefit of their skills, experience and time.

Dick Caddy, former Works Manager at W.C. Henderson & Son Printers Ltd., has proved to be a trusted companion and colleague. He sifted through numerous drafts of this manuscript, expertly correcting my technical writing errors with precision, firmness and tact.

Alex Paterson (local journalist for over 50 years) has proved to be a fount of knowledge from which I've frequently drawn. The fact that he appears on numerous pages in the text is proof that he has given a great deal to St Andrews over many years. Despite his deserved honours and his gentlemanly conduct at all times he is never condescending, regarding himself as a local who has not forgotten his roots.

Dr John Thompson (graduate of the University and Rector of Madras College for twenty years) has been a tremendous encouragement and a fair critic, reading and analysing this manuscript with canny insight and thoroughness.

Robert Smart (of St Andrews University Library and Muniments) maintains an unassuming stance which does not hide his widely acknowledged skills. I am only one of the latest, in a long line of authors, who has benefitted from his experience, insight and helpfulness.

When this book was first conceived, Dr Ronald Cant sowed some priceless seeds in my young writer's mind. My wife, parents and a few close friends have constantly encouraged me to persevere amongst the vagaries and doubts of a long period of germination.

The photographs which illustrate the text and captions have been kindly lent to the author for this publication only. Permission to re-use them lies with the individual copyright holders and *not* with the author or the publishers of this book.

The owners of the photographs are:
St Andrews University Library who authorised the publication of the many
prints chosen from the George M. Cowie Collection.
The Byre Theatre Company Limited; Tad Kucharski; Press Photographer:
William Flett; Alex Gourlay; David Niven, MBE; Ken Reid; Collector;
B. Solden; Photographer: Colin Ruscoe, 'Makarsbield', Tayport;
Eric Auchterlonie; Peter Adamson; Richard Govan; Mabel and Kenneth Ness;
Alex Paterson; J. Anderson; Mr Ralph Martin;
and The Old St Andrews Gallery.
Peter Adamson and his team at the University Photographic Unit have been
consistently generous with both their advice and co-operation in the
reproduction of original prints.

Contents

Introduction

JOHN MENZIES (1839-1905), my maternal great, great grandfather, came to St Andrews from Crieff to take up the position of Head Clerk at the newly opened railway station in 1887. In 1890 his wife was appointed as the caretaker-operator of the town's first telephone exchange which was situated in a room above Davy Grieve's tobacconist shop at 93 Market Street.

My father, Gordon Lyle, came to live in St Andrews during the 1950s when he married Elisabeth Menzies and they set up their own newsagency and fancy-goods business in the shop of the late Trochie Fleming at 45 South Street.

I was born in my grandparents' home on the Lade Braes, was educated at Madras College, married a Cupar lass fifteen years ago and we both continue to work in St Andrews where we have our home.

Shadows of St Andrews Past is a partial, but detailed, account of some of the people, places, events, institutions and the moods of the town and its community during the past century and beyond. By using my exclusive collection of recordings of local people's memories, collected rare photographs and the research of dusty books, brochures and old newspapers I have been able to recreate essential aspects of the community's latter history. Such local history undergirds the basis of modern St Andrews: both the people and their town. It is not an exaggeration to state that the subject-matter of this book could very easily have been forgotten with the passing of time and the older generations.

So many irrevocable changes have occurred within St Andrews during the period covered by this book that it seems worthwhile, I would say essential, to preserve the memory of that which has gone before, that which will never return, both for our own pleasure and for the benefit of future generations.

It is sobering to realise that elderly members of the community clearly remember the days when horse power was, literally, the only means of transportation in the town. Even at the turn of the century there remained abject poverty and squalid living conditions for too many of the populace, for Council Houses were not built before 1921 in St Andrews and the mass of private housing estates, built in the 1960s, were still under acres of farmland.

Shops were run by family concerns, often a rare bunch of characters, whilst the community of about 8,000 knew each other well. Tourists had started coming to St Andrews in the 1850s, living in palatial hotels from where they would golf and putt, tour the mediaeval ruins, swim from the sands and delight in the uniqueness of the historic old town.

Within a lifespan the character of St Andrews and its people has been transformed, making this book's publication imperative in order that locals, both old and new, and our welcome tourists, may appreciate our town's community history with accuracy. I am pleased that a truly local author, a fifth-generation St Andrean, has been enabled to record and recreate portions of the former things; things which belong to the heritage of his own community, bringing them out into the light of today from amongst the vague memories that make up the *Shadows of St Andrews Past.*

David W. Lyle
12 St Nicholas Street
St Andrews
Fife

The Lammas Market

IN THE MIDDLE AGES the Burgh of St Andrews held five annual market-fairs, although today, only one remains: The Lammas Market, which is the oldest surviving mediaeval market in Scotland. All five of the St Andrews markets originated from 1153 when King Malcolm gave his royal permission for the town to hold them on 'holy days' from the Church's calendar of Saints' Days.

The first of the yearly markets was the largest, named the Senzie Fair — held in April — lasting fifteen days. During this great

The Lammas Market tailed off at the west end of South Street, as viewed from atop the West Port looking east, at the beginning of this century. In those days the ploughmen and other farmworkers congregated at the 'Port' before walking as a group to the front of the Royal Hotel (next to Madras College East). There the feeing — the bargaining for terms of employment — between farmers and prospective workers took place.

market-fair the St Andrews harbour and the Eden Port nearby were filled with hundreds of ships. They had sailed from around the Scottish coast, England, France and the Low Countries. Merchants and traders unloaded their goods at the harbour and entered the Priory precincts through the Sea Gate. They carted their loads up the Pends Road before turning into the Cathedral's cloistered area where the Senzie and the other fairs were held.

At Senzie-time the visitors to St Andrews brought with them items such as linen, silk tapestries, carpets, spices, olive oil, armour, metal goods as well as pieces crafted in gold

By 1870 the trading aspect had declined and the Lammas Market took on the flavour of a fun-fair with a variety of booths, stalls and a few mechanical rides which were powered by steam-engine. Locals and farm people came into the town's main street in droves and enjoyed two days of merriment. This early form of the Lammas Market fun fair is captured here at the centre of South Street with the Town Hall on the right.

and silver. Local farmers and traders joined them to deal in grain, fish, arable crops, wool, skins, livestock and pottery goods.

The second annual market, held at St Andrews' cathedral precincts in the Middle Ages, took place on Trinity Day in June — followed on the first of August by the Lammas Market, being the Feast of St Peter ad Vincula. The fourth market was held on the second day of Michaelmas at the end of September, whilst the fifth annual market took place on the thirtieth November, the day of Saint Andrew.

The sole remaining descendant of those five ancient market-fairs is the Lammas (or

This 1902 photograph shows the Town Band playing on a platform at the west door of the Town Kirk in Church Square beside the City Hall (now the District Library) and old Logies Lane. The farm folk would dance away, the men in their tight suits and ties, while the women wore long dark dresses, frilly blouses and boater hats. The Lammas dancing ceased when the feeing left St Andrews for Cupar in 1915. There was an attempted revival of the dancing by locals in the 1930s but it didn't last.

In 1905 the South Street market was joined by a fair in Market Street comprising purely a fun-fair with the large rides of the period entering the street on the Thursday evening to set up. They operated during Friday and Saturday, closed on Sunday and were joined by the larger South Street market on the Monday and Tuesday. This photograph of the new Market Street fair in 1905 shows the popular horse-carousel sitting in front of Jimmy MacGregor's shop opposite Church Street. The carousel was powered by a steam-engine whilst children gathered round in their 'Sunday best'.

Mr James F. MacGregor (1870—1938) enjoyed the reputation of being the best-informed man on the subject of local affairs in St Andrews. During forty-five years Jimmy MacGregor auctioned the Market stances in South Street each Lammas Monday morning and he became a firm friend of the visiting showmen. Jimmy was the son of Provost John MacGregor; he was educated at Madras College before entering his father's diverse business which included farming, undertaking, painting and decorating, and auctioneering from their Market Street premises.

Loaf Mass) Market. It is now held on the second Monday in August, having lost all its religious significance during the Protestant Reformation. That was when the Lammas Market moved from the cathedral's cloistered precinct into the wide processional South Street which began at the Pends but had only latterly been extended to the newly-built West Port. The divorce of the August market from its former religious meaning was underlined by George Bruce, the mid-nineteenth century writer and town councillor. He wrote of the 1861 market: 'Several so-called ministers of the Gospel and some would-be layers, so forgot themselves as to try, by preaching and praying and singing psalms on a Lammas Market Day, to evangelise the motley and

This photograph shows the usual crowd of interested locals and showmen who always gathered around Jimmy MacGregor as he auctioned the stances in South Street. This is the Monday morning of the 1929 Lammas Market. The building behind him is the shop premises of Smith and Govan, the former chemist (taken over by Boots in the early 1930s) next door to Birrel's sweetshop with its striped sunshade.

merry crowd of human beings assembled that day'. He concluded his criticism of the religionists by quoting Scripture at them: 'As Solomon said, "There is a time and a place for everything under the sun" '.

The once popular 'swingboats' lost favour in the 1920s although a few specimens such as this one carried on until the early fifties. The swingboats were self-operated by the two passengers in each boat pulling a bound rope which determined the speed and height of their swing. Children were beginning to prefer the large mechanical rides to the old-fashioned swingboats, seen here outside the Fairfield Store in Market Street.

This is a typical George Cowie photograph, taken in 1937, from the roof of the Albert Buildings. The people below throng the stalls and rides of the Lammas Market in South Street with the Town Hall on the corner.

The Fishing Community

IN THE DIM AND DISTANT PAST before tourism arrived in the nineteenth century, before golf had superseded archery, before the university dons set foot in this cathedral city, before the magnificence of the cathedral and its wealthy priory reigned supreme, before the battlemented castle stood on its clifftop site, even before the Culdee monks settled around their church on the promontory; before anyone else lived in the area there existed a small fishing community. They were a sub-Pictish people who sustained a crude but self-sufficient lifestyle by fishing in the tempestuous bay, working

A group of St Andrews fishermen are pictured at the top of North Castle Street in 1910, only a few years before their living and community were irretrievably lost. These men, with weatherbeaten faces, full of character, were always glad to spend time relaxing onshore, but their sea-life was rarely out of mind.

on the uncultivated land and hunting the wild boar in the surrounding woodlands.

These first settlers lived in the area that, one day, would be a part of the town, piously named St Andrews. They lived at Woodburn, around the mouth of the Kinness Burn which flows into the modern harbour. By the 1150s, when the ecclesiastical authorities decided to build their cathedral at the hamlet of St Andrews, the small fishing community had moved up to the Fishergate area. They lived in a warren of wooden buildings situated in one of the oldest parts of the mediaeval town.

The harbour was first built *circa* 1100 around the basin of the tidal Kinness Burn,

This 1864 photograph shows two ninety-foot 'coasters' at St Andrews' inner harbour. They were delivering goods to the warehouse, seen on the right, at the quayside. The building, which sat in front of the Victorian gas works, was half-warehouse and half a human warren of cramped fisherfolk homes. The gas works, which lay immediately in front of the cathedral's easterly wall, operated from 1835 until the 1960s.

between the East Bents and the seaward side of the east priory wall. Fishermen used the harbour alongside the cargo vessels which brought in goods for the priory, the cathedral and later the growing number of merchants who came to live and work in the town. The harbour is first mentioned in official records in 1388 when pirates were harassing some of the cargo vessels heading for St Andrews. The pier was not built until several centuries later. At first it was of timber and only half the size of the present pier. This early pier collapsed during a terrible storm in December 1655. The following year a replacement was built, comprising stones from the abandoned cathedral and materials bought with monies raised by the sale of roofing lead and timber taken from the deserted castle.

The St Andrews fishing fleet gradually grew and by the end of the sixteenth century there was a well-established fishing community

The inappropriately named 'Royal George' warehouse and fisher-homes building, next to the quayside of the outer harbour and the old stone pier beyond, overlooks the cluster of small fishing 'yells' which were common at St Andrews whilst the fishing was flourishing. In this photograph some of the skippers and men are seen preparing for their next trip out before the high tide passes. The local fishermen would sail out into the squally St Andrews Bay to catch haddock, plaice, flounders or mackerel, depending on the season.

The missionary to the fishing community (in bowler hat) stands with three of his congregation, retired fishermen: Tam Eye, Johnnie Martin and Peter Cunningham. This photograph was taken in 1893 outside the mission hall in Gregory Place which once doubled as the original Fisher School until the Parish Council built the school building (now demolished) on Kirkhill in the 1870s. The fishermen's missionary held regular Gospel services, and conducted fisher weddings and funerals as well as bringing pastoral care to the fishing community.

Fisherwomen spent much of their time out on the streets of the Ladyhead in preference to their cramped living quarters. The women undertook most of the net-mending, fish-gutting and baiting of the lines for their men at sea. This 19th-century scene was quite typical with fisherwomen sitting on stools, working on the pavements along east North Street. The area, once known as the 'Fishergate', became the modern 'Ladyhead'.

with its quarter at the east end of North Street and the side streets that make up Castle Street. During the mid-eighteenth century a multiple tragedy occurred when the local fleet was fatally caught by a sudden storm in St Andrews Bay. Many fishermen were lost that day and for many years after that fisherfolk went to work on the land and in the town, causing a temporary cessation of most local fishing.

To a St Andrean it seems incongruous that, for over sixty years, local fishermen spurned the sea-life which had been their living. However, the fishing community were haunted by the memory of that day, in 1745, when the five large yawls from St Andrews

The fisherfolk spent more time outside their homes than in because there was hardly room inside their but-an-ben accommodation. The fishing community dominated the Ladyhead area and every inch was used to support the actual fishing done by the men. The women always wore the attractive traditional dress. Their saving relief from unremitting deprivation was their close-knit community lifestyle and the fact that they knew no other.

were smashed to pieces. Without warning, they were caught by a vicious storm out in the Bay and only a few men survived the tragedy.

In 1803 the Town Council arranged for a new fleet, men and their families, to join the reluctant fishing community of St Andrews. The newcomers came down from Shetland and were welcomed by their fellow fisher-people because they infused new life and expectancy after sixty years of uncanny fear. The coming of the new fishing fleet coincided with a period of increased coastal trade which helped to boost the local economy and the recently near-redundant harbour became a place of thronging activity.

Until the beginning of the 1900s this cluster of boats in the inner harbour was a familiar sight. Fishing vessels of all descriptions lie at rest during a low tide, sitting under the gaze of the distant cathedral towers.

This is the last St Andrews lifeboat The John and Sarah Hatfield, *being rowed from the outer harbour along by the pier to the open sea for a practice run. A number of fishing drifters can be seen at the quayside with one larger vessel resting after a fishing trip as the oar-powered lifeboat glides sedately past.*

This George Cowie portrait of old David Fenton captures the rugged character of a man who knew the sea well. He began his working life as a St Andrews fisherman, but when the local fishing was dying out he went up North for a time to continue his occupation. He returned to St Andrews in 1921 to work for the Town Council whilst also remaining a faithful member of the lifeboat crew, eventually becoming its coxswain during its last years in service. David Fenton witnessed the tail-end of the thriving fishing era at St Andrews, the dispersal of the fishing community and the void that remained thereafter.

Peter Waters was born at the Ladyhead in 1851; he was a burly fellow with a big heart who grew up and lived amongst the bustling fishing community of St Andrews. He was a skipper of his own fishing vessels until he retired aged seventy-three.

Joan (pronounced Joanne) was an exceptional character. She was born, bred and lived amongst the fishing community and always wore the distinctive clothes of a fisherwoman whilst she sold fresh fish from her barrow to townspeople. She wheeled her handcart through the old town centre and to the outlying houses from St Mary's Street round to Argyle Street. Joan became a much-loved figure whom the townspeople adopted as their own. She would chat away to her customers, always a smile on her face, helping to banish the barriers that had existed between the fisher and town communities for centuries.

Harbourmaster Chisholm and his lad bring in a catch of mackerel at the base of the pier in 1932. They are watched by Peter Martin and John Downie, both former fishermen who became caddies. Since the 1930s all net fishing has ceased from St Andrews; the remaining local fishermen (fewer than ten today) use motor-powered boats to lay and retrieve their creels which catch lobster and crab for sale to fish shops and restaurants.

Sandy 'Sandshoes' Chisholm was born at the Ladyhead in 1883 and was a local fisherman. 'Sandshoes' was also a member of the lifeboat crew from 1902 until its disbandment in 1939.

Whilst other fishermen took to hiring-out rowing boats at the harbour, taking tourists around the Bay in their cruisers, or found work in the town, Sandy remained at the fishing until the 1940s when, finally, there was no more fishing to be done. He went to the golf course to become a well-known caddy on the St Andrews Links.

The Old Town

Rab Martin (1873-1931) proudly displays his grooming skills as he stands beside his horse and cart outside the West Port circa 1900. Rab was a local fish cadger. On the left can be seen part of Tam Marr's second bakery shop, which eventually closed in 1921. To the right is where, since 1938, Neil Westwood has had his tiny newsagent's shop in South Street, where Cody Wilson and Jimmy Marr were his predecessors. At the time of the photograph, however, a Mrs Caldwell owned the shop and ran it as a tobacconist's, hence the jars in the window.

Taken in 1902, this photograph looks along South Street towards the 16th-century West Port. A few years after this picture was taken the cobbles at either side of the rough roadway were replaced by tarmac; the giant Victorian flowerpots and old-style gas lamps were removed. Those were the days when shops were run by family concerns such as Coopers and Aikman & Terras, on the right here but hidden by the abundant trees that once lined South Street. During this period the occasional steam-powered engine may have traversed the roadway, but the combustion engine had not yet superseded the clippety-clop of the numerous horses pulling carts, brakes, carriages and cabs.

Snow brings a touch of magic to Market Street west in the 1930s. Shops are seen here which disappeared long ago; shops such as Currie the grocer, Duff the barber and Armit the baker (who also had a shop in Church Street). The cars of that vintage are collectors' items now although quite commonplace at the time. The ornate electric lamp and stand in the centre of St Andrews' main shopping street adds the final touch which makes this view of the old town something forever past.

(See opposite page)

This is how the market place of Market Street looked in 1909 with its Victorian desecration, in the form of the fountain, erected as a memorial to the local golfing gentleman and little-known author Whyte-Melville. Originally the Mercat Cross was positioned there in memory of those who were martyred for heresy. The fountain ceased to function many decades ago and has since been maintained as a glorified plant-pot. The Mercat Cross was regularly surrounded by local traders on market days and that tradition is carried on by a few local people selling anything from plants and flowers to books and bric-a-brac.

This 1864 photograph looks down North Street from the east along the cobbled roadway. Fisher-homes are on the right, being the tip of the Ladyhead, next to the Episcopal church which stood behind the wall and railings from 1825 until 1869. The church building was removed stone by stone to a site down the coast when the congregation moved to the Queen's Terrace site of today. That area and the site where the old house is seen here were built over in the 1950s to accommodate the University's administrative offices named College Gate. St Salvator's Tower stands tall whilst the former Martyrs Church steeple rises on the left of the photograph. North Street was quieter then, with a child going shopping, wandering in the middle of the road, and a cab strolling along in the distance.

This is old Union Street as it stood before the entire west side was demolished in the 1930s. This west side was once the site of the town rubbish dump and it was then called Foul Waste until these houses were built in 1846. At the end of the row of houses sits the formerly well-known building called the Double Decker, seen here from the rear. The Double Decker was so named because of its twin set of dormer windows on its roof. It contained a row of small shops on its ground floor frontage with roomy housing on the floors above. These houses were condemned as slums by the Town Council in the early 1930s. All the tenants were rehoused in the new council houses of Boase Avenue. The business premises seen on the far side of Market Street belonged to Carmine Palompo who had his sweet shop and fish restaurant there.

This is a part of St Andrews that many
incomers and tourists don't see. The town
has always had a riddle of lanes, closes and
wynds criss-crossing its centre. This 1930s
photograph has captured the 17th-century
houses of Loudens Close which is on a 'rig'
adjacent to western South Street. This was
the first property that the St Andrews
Preservation Trust restored. The outside toilets
have gone, as has the old gas lamp shown in
this pre-restoration photograph.

This is a tranquil view of Golf Place in the early 1900s, the only traffic consisting of a horse and cart (the driver off-loading goods at the former Links Hotel) and another, just discernible in the distance on the right, crawling up the road. This picture reminds us that St Andrews has been a tourist town since the 1840s. So many of its old hotels have gone: the Athol; the Alexandra; the Star; the Crown; the Golf; the Imperial; the Crosskeys; the Royal; and the Westpark Hotel. The Grand Hotel, one of the more palatial establishments for monied tourists, was built in 1896, and royalty patronised its best suites which overlooked both the famous 'Old' golf course and the West Sands. The hotel was sold to the University in 1949 (causing a huge outcry from many local people who felt that the University had taken over enough buildings of the town) as a hall of residence.

This is old Abbey Court as it looked in the 1920s. These houses were built in 1852 on land where previously corn barns, a brewery and a canvas factory stood. Old Abbey Court was demolished in the mid-sixties to allow for the 1970 construction of the present Abbey Court comprising council flats grouped, on two storeys, around a courtyard of garages. Looking from the photograher's position today you will see the wall, on the left, running right up Byre Wynd which goes past the side of modern Abbey Court on its right, past the new Byre Theatre, through Southcourt into South Street.

This photograph depicts something of the squalor that the fisher-people of St Andrews had to endure at the turn of the century. The building was inappropriately named 'The Royal George' (after a famous steamship), but this half-warehouse/half human warren of fisher-homes was anything but royal. The people who lived there could savour the odours of the harbour when the tide was out on the one side and the gas works on the other just behind the house on the right of this picture. The building had originally been a series of warehouses until the 1850s when the major portion was reconstructed into but-an-ben fisherfolk accommodation with a grocer's shop at the front and a pub at each end of the building.

The Old Byre Theatre

THE BYRE THEATRE at St Andrews celebrated its fiftieth birthday in 1983. Today, there is a modern purpose-built theatre building in Abbey Street which contains: a sizeable foyer, box office and administrator's office; a bar lounge, a coffee lounge and gallery; a spacious auditorium and a large stage with up-to-date technical facilities to match. There are fair-sized dressing rooms, a 'green room', a technician's room and storage. Throughout the years the Byre Theatre (affectionately known simply as the 'Byre') had continued its half-century run because both amateurs and professionals had always worked as a team. Actors and volunteers performed, directed, pulled

Alex B. Paterson poses for George Cowie in the Old Byre Theatre's small auditorium. He led the founder members of the St Andrews Play Club which was formed in 1933. The Club went on to establish the Byre Theatre with Alex Paterson as its volunteer administrator — ultimately for almost forty years. He wrote dozens of local plays, and directed, produced and even acted occasionally at the Byre. Alex (A.B.) Paterson was a well-known and busy freelance journalist who gave a great deal of time and energy to take the Byre Theatre through its many struggles as a small repertory theatre into the 1970s when it was moved into the modern, purpose-built theatre of today. Presently, he is Chairman of the Byre Theatre Company Ltd., remaining a driving force, determined never to be merely a figurehead.

This is Carstair's former Abbey Street dairy farm as it looked in the Winter of 1933 when the Play Club applied to the Town Council for a temporary let of the condemned building. Despite the mess of the former cow stalls and the rotting potatoes that had been stored there latterly, the amateur Play Club decided that this was to be the venue for their drama studio which, shortly afterwards, became the first Byre Theatre: the only theatre in St Andrews.

The converted cowshed was made into a unique and pretty little repertory theatre, the only such establishment in St Andrews. The old ship's ladder, which the Play Club purchased from Inverkeithing Docks, is seen on the left leading to the attic rooms, whilst the main entrance to the tiny foyer is sited at the right-hand corner.

This photograph shows the west portion of the old Byre's auditorium with an evening audience entranced by a performance by a professional company. Both the amateurs and professionals performed great feats on the miniature stage which was never enlarged during the theatre's history.

'Its fame is indeed out of all proportion to its size.' *Pictured here are actors in the tiny attic dressing-room, making up for a performance of* As You Like It *in 1947. The facilities were always minimal in both size and provision; it is a credit to the actors and actresses that they coped so well despite such limitations. They were able to adapt fully and provide excellent entertainment. The dressing rooms and the 'Green Room' where the actors met were all in the attic of the Byre; the atmosphere had to be friendly, indeed there was always a close camaraderie amongst Company members.*

Here we view the south-west portion of old Abbey Street about to be demolished. The large gap is the site where the new Byre Theatre was to be built, with the old Byre sitting just to the front of the Morris Minor car. Beyond that is the site of the demolished old Abbey Court with the former Crown Hotel peeking out at the left of the photo which was taken by Andrew Cowie in October 1968.

together in building sets, assisting in the distribution of tickets, programmes and posters. Together they sold refreshments, ushered in the audience, cleaned the theatre, repaired costumes and hunted out props from townspeople.

However, it is acknowledged by all that one man has been the inspiration, the guiding and leading spirit of the Byre from the beginning. This man is the former administrator, director, playwright and presently the Chairman of the Board of Trustees, Alex B. Paterson. Alex was born and brought up in the town, his profession being *the* area journalist for over fifty years. In 1958 he was awarded the MBE by the Queen, in 1970 he received an 'oscar' from STV for his services to Scottish Theatre, and in that same year St Andrews University

conferred on him their first Honorary Degree of Master of Arts. Ann Gibson, an actress who worked at the Byre between 1956 and 1959, visited St Andrews recently and said of Alex, 'He had the ability to generate high achievements from average actors and he was on first-name terms with them all'. Looking back, Alex himself believes that the Byre was a natural development which emerged from within the town rather than something that was imposed from outside and that its foundation coincided with a national revival of interest in the theatre.

Who's Afraid of Virginia Woolf? Edward Albee's modern classic performed during the last season at the old Byre in 1969. The fabric of the theatre was allowed to run down because the new theatre's opening was approaching, with all funds going to that, whilst the demolition of the old Byre was imminent. However, the Company played on; here we see the producer, Anthony Matheson (standing), Michael Sanderson and Carole Boyd in rehearsal during the last days of the old theatre.

Alex Paterson takes a last look at the old Byre Theatre building in January 1970 just before it was demolished to make way for new Council housing. All that remains of the old Byre is the doocot that was originally in the wall of the steading and is now on the Abbey Street frontage of the new Byre Theatre.

Golf Clubmakers

WHEN THE WORLD'S FIRST professional golfer, Allan Robertson of St Andrews, reluctantly bridged the gap between the era of the feathery and the gutta percha golf ball, he was in the company of skilled local craftsmen who no longer made crude bludgeons for the playing of gowff. They had progressed to creating elegant handmade golf clubs in beech, apple, pear and other suitable indigenous hardwoods. Indeed James Pett of St Andrews was supplying the Marquis of Montrose with golf clubs in 1672, clubmaking being his full-time occupation. At the beginning of the 1700s Henry Mill was a local clubmaker as well as being the official supplier of clubs to St Andrews University. David Dick, who lived and had his workrooms in College Street, was also a noted clubmaker until his death in 1731. Back in 1506 records tell us that hand-crafted clubs could cost 1/- each, but the price rose, as did the local industry, which came to the fore from the early 1800s through to the beginning of this century.

Hugh Philip started his working life as a joiner and decorator who mended golf clubs in his spare time. By September 1819 he was

This is a rare collection of golf clubs from the R. & A.'s museum. These old-timers were all handmade and would have been commissioned by individuals for their own use. Today this range of strange clubs would be illegal in competition golf.

acknowledged to be highly proficient in the skill and he was employed by the Society of Golfers to undertake all their repairs and orders for new clubs. He left his Argyle Street premises to set up a workshop in the Union Parlour in Golf Place before finally moving to the building that was later to be the home, workshop and retail premises of Tom Morris.

Hugh Philip's chief assistant from 1845 to 1852, James Wilson, set up his own clubmaking establishment and retail shop at the old building which sat on the site of the 1887-built Rusack's Marine Hotel overlooking the eighteenth fairway. When Hugh Philip died in 1856 his nephew, Robert Forgan, succeeded him in the business, starting out with only one assistant, named Jamie Anderson. Anderson went on to win the Open Championship three times in succession. It was not long before Robert Forgan began to expand, employing more local men and training them in the craft. He also made a chance discovery, when a wrong load of wood was delivered to his workshop, that hickory was ideal for making club shafts, and from St Andrews its widespread use began.

St Andrews clubmakers remained in business until the late 1920s when the introduction of the mass-produced steel shaft made much of their true craftsmanship obsolete. Only Stewart, Forgan and Auchterlonie were able to continue, either because of their size or their ability to specialise.

Originally all golf clubs (and even balls at one time) were made of hardwoods until Allan Robertson commissioned a local blacksmith to make him a hooked iron implement (later known as a 'cleek' from the old Scots word for hook) for playing his ball out of the rough and from bunkers. The idea quickly caught on and local blacksmiths produced ever-increasing numbers of the new 'cleek' for golfers. Cleek-making was a distinct branch of clubmaking for many years as blacksmiths manufactured the new 'iron', whilst the traditional clubmakers carried on making their crafted wood clubs.

During the late 1800s Robert Wilson lived and worked at west North Street and he became known as *the* pioneer of a more refined shape of iron head which he produced from the most basic type to the niblick. His designs, which were created for the new gutta ball, became models for later master-blacksmiths and laid the foundations for the modern sets of irons. Robert White, meanwhile, a blacksmith by trade, ran the last commercial concern to use the mediaeval mill lade which went through his workshop at the foot of the Pends into the harbour nearby. A notable apprentice was Tom Stewart who subsequently started up his own famous 'Pipe Brand' cleek factory in Argyle Street. Condie of Market Street was another local blacksmith who concentrated mainly on cleek-making, whilst Spence and Gourlay, down beside the lifeboat station in Woodburn Place, were the first blacksmiths to team up with a clubmaker when they combined forces with Robert Forgan in 1920 to supplement the output from his own small cleek-making factory in Market Street.

The founder of 'Forgans', the largest clubmaking concern in St Andrews, both in the past and at present, was Robert Forgan who began by inheriting the business of his uncle, Hugh Philip, in 1856. Forgan's clubmaking skills were famous, so much so that H.R.H. The Prince of Wales, on being elected Captain of the R. & A. commissioned a set from him. Robert Forgan not only introduced hickory in the making of woods, but he discovered that implanting pegs to secure the bone soles of wooden clubs gave them greater durability. Robert Forgan was succeeded by his son Thomas who

introduced further innovations such as the 'bulger' driver and the 'Mellor's' putter. Forgan's main workshop was situated at Pilmour Links, overlooking the Old Course, whilst his cleek-making factory was sited behind 110 Market Street. The business at these premises employed up to nearly one hundred and fifty men at one time, including many time-served craftsmen.

It is a great credit to the local firms such as Stewarts', Auchterlonies' and Forgans' that their hand-crafted clubs were renowned throughout the world and that they drew as many golfers to St Andrews as the famous Old Course or the R. & A. Clubhouse ever did. The heyday of St Andrews golf

The founder of St Andrews' largest and longest-surviving golf clubmaking concern, Robert Forgan, is pictured here sitting (left) in his cleek-making factory at 110 Market Street in the 1880s.

clubmaking began in the days when golf clubs had their own identities. There were play or tee clubs, long, mid and short spoons, a baffing spoon, a driving putter and a wooden putter. In place of their numbered counterparts of today there were: bulgers, brassies, spoons, baffies, jiggers, mashies and niblicks.

The introduction, in 1929, of mass-produced golf clubs crushed the relatively

A portrait of a clever craftsman and an astute businessman in his old age. Robert Forgan began his working life as a joiner, working for his uncle who became a master-clubmaker named Hugh Philip. When his uncle died he was left a well-established and highly reputable small business. Starting with only one assistant, Robert Forgan built up his clubmaking concern into a world-famous business which was carried on by his son until 1962.

This photograph shows Jimmy Anderson, clubmaker, working in Forgan's workshop in Pilmour Place. Jimmy had started with Forgan at the age of fourteen, underwent his seven-year apprenticeship and remained with the firm until his retiral.

small businesses of St Andrews' clubmaking craftsmen. Many local clubmakers were forced to give up immediately, knowing that they could not compete with such large-scale, cost-efficient opposition from national companies. David and Willie Auchterlonie tried bravely to work on with the traditional methods — only to face liquidation in the 1930s. Forgans, with its mass-production element, carried on until the 'sixties. A national company bought Forgans, carrying on for less than a year until, in 1963, the new owners sold the building to the Woollen Mill and the machinery elsewhere; the large staff were abruptly paid off with skilled clubmakers finding themselves on the dole. Tom and Eric Auchterlonie were able to carry on, despite the massive inroads made by the mass-production companies, because their business had a healthy retail side as well as specialising in hand-made clubs such as their wooden-headed putter. For St Andreans golf is still the native game, but the days when clubmaking employed more locals than any other single industry are long gone.

The late Laurie Auchterlonie showing one of the antique clubs that he bought and sold, sometimes exhibiting them in his tiny museum which was the shop where his father and uncle (D. & W.) made and sold clubs until 1930. Laurie was an acknowledged expert on the subject of clubmaking and of antique clubs in particular. He followed in his father's footsteps by becoming the honorary professional to the Royal and Ancient in 1964. He was a specialist in piecing together a full set from a number of individual antique clubs, and only those with a lot of money could afford to purchase these rarities. He spent many years in America setting up the golf museum at Foxburg and he advised the Americans on all matters pertaining to golf. Laurie was the grandson of a local master-plumber and the son of Willie Auchterlonie who was the last St Andrews-born professional golfer to win the American Open, which he did in 1921.

The staff of Forgan's the golf clubmakers celebrating the Coronation in 1937, twenty-six years before the firm's demise. This photograph bears witness to the fact that no fewer than one-hundred and seventeen local people were employed by Forgan's during the period when other local clubmakers had to fold. Forgan's was truly a large company in St Andrews in 1930s terms, just as it would be in the present day.

This final photograph shows Forgan's golf clubmaking factory where the St Andrews Woollen Mill has its main saleroom today. Rows of skilled craftsmen and apprentices worked by a generous measure of daylight because the true colours of the grained wood, and the staining and the polishing could best be judged under such conditions. Forgan's was not only the largest clubmaking concern in St Andrews, nor just the longest surviving, but it also enjoyed a worldwide reputation. It was bought over as a going concern, in 1962, by a national company which closed down the works and paid off all the employees (from craftsmen to cleaners) within the year, and in 1963 the property was sold to a wholly unrelated business.

Events

The Princess Wilhelmina *from Halmnsted in Sweden languishes on the West Sands on September 29th, 1912. She had been caught by a storm in St Andrews Bay and had sent out a distress flare as she drifted towards the rocks below the Castle. The St Andrews lifeboat rescued her nine-man crew before the strong tide carried the empty vessel away from the rocks due west onto the West Sands. Local people were up at dawn scavenging the crewless ship, climbing the mast and looking inside the ship, and someone had brought a cart to take away their pickings.*

On the students' Charities Day of 1958 paper footprints were to be seen climbing up the hallowed St Salvator's Tower. The Quaestor and Factor of the University contacted local tradesman Willie Fulton and asked if he could remove the offending footprints. 'Na buther', said Willie, who requisitioned tackle, a bosun's chair and the assistance of Bill Humphries. When Willie was putting his gear into position some students appealed to him to leave the footprints alone, but Willie was determined to see the job through. He swung off the top of the tower, secure in the chair, lowered slowly by Bill who was guiding the 'lead' rope below. All was going well until the students got hold of the 'lead' rope, took it into the Old Union next door and locked themselves in. Thus Willie was captured on film hanging several yards from the tower, helpless for the whole afternoon. It turned out that the students had bribed Bill with a fiver (about a week's wages then) to give them the rope. Willie was fair annoyed at the time, but looking back, he just laughs about that unforgettable Charities Day of over thirty years ago.

The local British Legion branch marches along the middle of South Street in the 1930s. This is a sight not seen now, but between the Boer War and the Second World War the Legion were a very active organisation in St Andrews. They first hired premises at 105 South Street before they rented the old malt barns and rooms above at Wilson's Brewery in Argyle Street. There they had social rooms and an extensive rifle-range. They were eventually given the former church of St Mary's, since known as the Victory Memorial Hall, in St Mary's Place. The Legion offered ex-servicemen recreational pastimes and they held social functions such as laying on a meal for the unemployed of the town.

The St Andrews Horse Parade began each year with the showing of beautifully groomed and gaily decorated working horses which were in the care of farm labourers and ploughmen. The event was held in the cobbled Market Street Square outside MacGregor's shop. The horses were judged and the winners presented with their trophies. Here is James Horsburgh, the winner of the Scott Memorial Cup for the best animal in the parade at the 1936 event.

(See opposite page)

On Hogmanay, before midnight, each year hundreds of locals assembled outside the Post Office in South Street during the first half of this century. There was dancing, and singing, and the local pipe band marched and played. Six minutes before 1936 dawned this group of revellers awaited the midnight chimes. Kneeling is 'Tip' Anderson, who could be counted on to be over fu' that night (and most others), but he used to lead the dancing with great gusto. Everyone knew 'Tip': he'd been a local carter and became a noted caddy. When the Kirk bells tolled midnight, the gathered company wished each other 'a guid new year' before setting off to first-foot around the town. Sadly this community event faded out in the early 1950s.

The prizegiving ceremony at the St Andrews Annual Horse Parade took place in Market Street from a float with the competitors surrounding the area. The event was originally started to encourage farm workers to take a greater care and pride in their horses. After the prizegiving the horses proceeded down Church Street, along South Street, through the West Port and along Argyle Street to Cockshaugh Park where large numbers of local people went to see the parading horses and the gymkhana that took place afterwards. This once-popular event died out after 1952 because the farm horses were being superseded by the tractor.

The crowd at a Horse Parade Day gymkhana at Cockshaugh Park.

The Victorian, iron-constructed, St Andrews bandstand lies in the natural hollow, called the Bow Butts, beside Witch Hill, between the Royal and Ancient clubhouse and the entrance to the former Step Rock pool. Local people would flock to the bandstand on Sunday afternoons to listen to the bands which came to play there including the town's own City Silver Band. Crowds would gather around the top of the surrounding mound which was naturally terraced by the cattle which had once grazed there. In summer both locals and visitors stood around the bandstand, or they could hire a deckchair from the Step Rock attendant. The Bow Butts area was once the place where archery was practised in enforced preference to games like fitba' or gowff. The sport was practised at the Bow Butts and competitions with medals and trophies to be won were regularly held there. Archery was superseded by golf in the early 1800s, and then the bandstand was built for the amusement and recreation of the local people. In recent years the bandstand was hardly used at all and it was allowed to decay. The Community Council and local people made a plea to the District Council who have since refurbished and repainted it. Today there is a modest revival of bands playing there on Sundays during the summer months, with local school bands taking the lead.

This photograph by Andrew Cowie was taken on 4th December 1969. Workmen look on as the Crown Hotel receives its burial as part of the Council's road-widening scheme when the whole east side of old Abbey Street was razed to the ground. The street was once known as Abbey Wynd and was one of the first streets of the early town where farmworkers generally lived. Until its demolition it was a narrow street with houses hidden behind the frontage, and whilst it could be considered quaint, the accommodation had become sub-standard and squalid, hence the need for demolition to make way for a wider and more suitable trunk road and a walkway amidst a greenbelt. The Crown Hotel (formerly the Crown Inn) stood exactly opposite the houses which were demolished to make way for the new Byre Theatre in Abbey Street west. The Crown dated back to the 17th century and was next door to a former inn which had been established in the Middle Ages. The Crown had retained its former stables and courtyard which were used latterly for car parking.

On the Saturday following the annual Kate Kennedy procession students used to take to the town's main streets again in a much less respectful manner. They paraded on twelve floats for charity. Each float was decorated to a theme by the students of various halls of residence. They gathered at St Salvator's Quad for the judging to find the most original float. Thereafter they held a hectic and jocular parade around the streets. In the 1960s local youngsters started bombarding the hapless student floats with pea-shooters, which were enjoying a revival. The following year the students were ready for them with bags of flour and water. It was great fun, but the Senate took a dim view of developments, and so the Charities parades of the early 1970s were much reduced. This annual event finally folded after the 1985 procession chiefly because, the year before, Wilson's bottling company had closed and its lorries were sold off. Wilson's had always willingly lent the students its whole fleet for the Charities Day parade. The event in 1985 was a poor reflection of its former self and the students wisely decided that it could not carry on. In the days of the parades the floats would finish their journey at Kinburn Park where a fair was held and youngsters could climb up on the floats. Today, a fair is still held at Kinburn Park but it is a mere shadow of the days when it was preceded by the parade.

It was a dismal, wet day in St Andrews on Wednesday 23rd October 1940 when Prime Minister Winston Churchill came to the area to inspect the Polish Forces who were defending the coast from enemy attack. The threat of invasion was very real and the coastal defences were undertaken with military secrecy and precision — a story in itself. After a civic reception at Cupar, Churchill travelled by car to St Andrews before he, his wife and General Sikorski, Commander-in-Chief of the exiled Polish Forces in Britain, made a tour of inspection. They walked along the West Sands to inspect the soldiers on duty, the concrete blocks that would deter an amphibious landing, and the tall wooden stakes in the sands to prevent enemy planes landing on the long beach.

Churchill was in buoyant spirits as he tramped over the dunes. A local woman approached him with an autograph book in her hand; an aide tried to stop her approaching the Prime Minister, but Churchill waved him aside to happily give his autograph to her and to many others that day. Churchill and Sikorski inspected a Polish Guard of Honour while a military band played the British and Polish national anthems. It later transpired that Churchill was so impressed by the Polish force at St Andrews that they were the first Scottish coastal defence battalion to receive more tanks, guns and ammunition on his orders. Churchill is pictured above saluting the Polish soldiers along the West Sands with General Sikorski standing proudly nearby.

This unique picture of Winston Churchill was taken by a local photographer. It is still Wednesday 23rd October, 1940 and Churchill, waiting for the next train, nonchalantly reads the Times *newspaper at St Andrews railway station.*

The Step Rock

THE CHARMING OLD COVE where the actual Step Rock stands had been a favourite area for men and boys to swim in from the eighteenth to the twentieth centuries. This was first confirmed by the provision of a Victorian bathing shelter, erected each spring from 1873 beside the Rock. In 1903 the grand, 300-foot long, Step Rock Pool was constructed, running from the beach and out to the sea beside the central attraction of the cove: The Rock. In the 1930s proper shelters and huts were built to form the Step Rock Complex when women were allowed to join the men there.

This photograph, taken in 1874, shows holidaymakers looking out from the former Scores path to the undeveloped Step Rock area. Bathers are swimming beside the Step Rock which once lay below the eroded Witch Hill. In the far distance mobile bathing carriages sit along the West Sands with the Links running behind the beach.

The Step Rock Amateur Swimming Club gave a full service to local swimmers with their classes, competitions, life-savers and galas. They mediated on behalf of swimmers with the Town Council and they were largely responsible for the early development of the Step Rock Complex. They encouraged the social side of life which was based at the Step Rock, giving pleasure and freedom to both local and visiting youth.

The progressive Step Rock Club were the first to call for an indoor pool in the town. Only after fifty years was a modern pool built, but again the town's swimming club were in the middle of the campaign which yielded the late 1980s provision of a Leisure Centre incorporating a four-lane, 25-metre-long main pool, a 50-metre water-chute and a toddlers' pool. The modern sports and leisure facilities in the same building as the Pool Hall are a boon to both townspeople and tourists. However, there remain hundreds of locals and visitors, spread over many generations, who will never forget the many hours of healthy fun and lasting pleasure that the crowded 'Steppie' once gave them.

This is one of the first swimming galas held at the Step Rock. It is 1909 and there is a small refreshments kiosk on the left with the men's bathing station sitting beside the actual Step Rock. It overlooks the pool which had been built in 1903 and measured 300 feet by 100 feet.

Some familiar St Andrews faces are to be found amongst this group of the Step Rock Amateur Lifeguard Corps. The club was founded in 1928 with the object of promoting the art of swimming, competition swimming, diving, life-saving and aquatic sports. The club's badge was in a royal blue with the initials 'S.R.A.' embossed above a white Saint Andrew cross and it was worn on the chest area of both men's and women's costumes.

The Step Rock Amateurs club taught generations of youngsters to swim and led them on from the basics to life-saving, diving and competition swimming. Don't our hearts bleed for this young girl taking her first tentative strokes in the strange water at the Step Rock under the experienced supervision of senior club members.

The many galas held at the Step Rock brought thousands of spectators to watch the action in and around the pool. Bathing belle competitions were held along with serious swimming competitions, diving exhibitions, games of water polo and children's events on the popular gala days. The eager crowd in this photograph of 1934, awaiting the start of events, seem momentarily more interested in being captured by George Cowie's camera. The tiers of concrete and wood-built seats were prime viewing positions, but note the row of spectators behind the railings above, and it was a certainty that hundreds more would be crowded along the clifftop, the sands and around the pool, all trying to get a good view of the gala.

This 1940s photograph depicts a quieter Step Rock at sunset on a warm summer's evening after the crowds have left to enjoy social activities at cafes, dances and cinemas. The relative quiet of the Step Rock on a summer evening brings out the elderly, who sit in deckchairs on the beach, whilst children paddle in their pond and youngsters have the run of the main pool.

The Step Rock Club's cutter, for use by their lifeguard corps, to assist those in distress, whether swimmers or those in hired rowing boats around the shore. The cutter was brand-new and in May 1939, when it was bought it cost exactly £9.0s.0d.

Young people always gathered here, below the actual Step Rock, on the concrete platform which lay in front of the diving board and chute. Visitors and townspeople met and made friends there whilst enjoying a panoramic view of the pool and its complex from their favourite spot.

The Step Rock as it appeared in the early 1970s with very few people using the facility even in midsummer compared with the thronging crowds who spent long days there from the 1930s to the 1960s. This photo shows the toddlers' pool next to a portion of the main pool, with the terracing behind and to the left the dominating male changing block with the tiny pay-hut next door.

Those glorious summer days at the 'Steppie'
as it was in 1946.

Tom and Eric Auchterlonie

ERIC AUCHTERLONIE RETIRED from his unique brand of golf clubmaking in his native town of St Andrews at the beginning of 1986. This ended his family's almost one hundred years in the local trade which they first established behind his grandfather's plumber's workshop in 1894. The Auchterlonie name became famous for its superior workmanship and knowledge of experimental golf clubmaking. Never the largest of St Andrews firms, their quality craftsmanship alone ensured their fame, notably from the 1920s.

Eric's grandfather was a local master-plumber, named David Auchterlonie, who started his own business behind his home in Union Street in 1864. He and his wife had six sons and two daughters, all of whom he saw grow up before his death in 1915.

The six brothers were: Laurence, who won the United States Open Championship in 1902; David and Willie, who set up the first Auchterlonies' golf clubmaking firm in St Andrews; John, who followed his father as a plumber in St Andrews; Joe, initially apprenticed as a plasterer but later switched to clubmaking; the youngest of the brothers was Tom who was born in 1879. Tom

This was formerly the building used by Richard Wilson as his furniture store in Fleming Place. Tom Auchterlonie bought it in 1921 and converted it into a sizeable clubmaking workshop whilst maintaining his retail premises in Ellice Place.

(See opposite page)

This 1917 photograph shows Tom Auchterlonie (second from left) with the clubmakers of his brothers' firm of D. & W. Auchterlonie outside their shop at 4 Pilmour Links. The workshop was situated behind their father's plumber's business in east Union Street. The firm folded in 1936, leaving Willie alone to continue selling retail goods with only one clubmaker working with him at the back of the shop. Willie Auchterlonie was born in 1872; he played in the British Open Championship at the age of sixteen when Jack Burns won the title over the Old Course. Five years later, in 1893, Willie won the championship. His equipment on that occasion comprised a set of seven clubs which he had made himself. In September 1935 Willie was appointed honorary professional to the Royal and Ancient Golf Club where he carried out his duties with courteous efficiency. He was also responsible for laying out the Jubilee Course which was opened in 1946. In 1956 he was made an Honorary Member of the R. & A.; he died at the age of ninety-one in 1964. His son, Laurie, who was best known for his golf-related work in America, became the R. & A.'s Honorary Professional after his father and in 1964 he made the former D. & W. shop into a small personal museum of antique clubs until his death.

underwent an operation when he was young which resulted in the shortening of one leg. He always had to wear a heightened stout boot to compensate for the shortening, but it never hindered him from playing golf with his brothers. One sister married a local clubmaker by the name of Jock Brown, whilst the other daughter remained single, living with and looking after her parents at their home.

Tom died at the age of eighty-three in 1963, having established his own successful clubmaking business in 1919, quickly gaining a high reputation for his individual craftsmanship. He trained Eric to be a skilled craftsman of golf clubs in his own right.

Pictured here is the west end of Tom Auchterlonie's workshop with some of his clubmakers, sandpapering heads and shafts; planing, scraping and filing; ready for staining, stamping, finishing off and polishing.

Whilst other St Andrews firms folded, Auchterlonie's carried on into the 1980s. Over the years Eric continued the family's clubmaking tradition but he chose to restrict it to a select and specialised form including his famous wooden-headed putters, many going abroad with others selling as commissioned trophies. The Auchterlonies could not, and never attempted to, compete against the larger local firms like Forgans and Stewarts, who both engaged in a certain amount of mass production. There was a time when Eric went around retailers to sell his own clubs, but he hated the task and had to be content with the services of a commission agent which never proved satisfactory, but it did allow Eric back to his first love of making specialist clubs. In the Golf Place shop Eric employed only two craftsmen who worked alongside him with up to five shop assistants in the faster turnover retail side.

During Tom and Eric's lifetime golf clubmaking was transformed by modern technology and mass production. However,

This portrait of Tom Auchterlonie was taken in 1919, the year that he risked all by setting up his own clubmaking business which proved to be the most astute move of his life.

This is the aviary that Tom Auchterlonie was responsible for having installed at Kinburn Park in the 1930s after long negotiations with the Town Council who owned the park. A wide variety of cagebirds have been on show there ever since, providing an added attraction for visitors to the park. Tom became a successful breeder of cagebirds and was a highly respected authority on canaries, whilst his services as a judge at top shows throughout the country were greatly in demand.

they continued to use only the basic
machinery of their trade, practising their
personal skills in the very best traditions of
golf clubmaking in St Andrews.

*Eric with his father in the Golf Place shop
after they had become partners in 1955. The
1919-established business was continued
after his father's death until Eric's retirement
in 1986.*

This photograph was taken in 1935 when the Auchterlonies first opened their Golf Place shop and clubmaking rooms. Eric and his wife lived in the house above until his retirement when he sold the business as a going concern. The unseen section of the building, to the right, was MacArthur's café and shop on two floors. Eric expanded his business by buying their property in the early 1960s. Today the business is run by a British firm who retain the Auchterlonie name with Eric retaining a directorship in an advisory capacity.

Tom Auchterlonie in retirement, aged eighty-two, in 1962. He is standing in Pilmour Links near his brothers' former shop, which he left in 1919 to set up his own successful and lasting business. In the background is the corner of the Golf Place shop which he had left in Eric's capable hands. Tom was a meticulous man in both clubmaking and bird-rearing and this element of industrious dedication proved to be the personal feature that secured the timeless reputation that the name of Auchterlonie enjoys in golf clubmaking circles to this day.

Characters

Donald Mitchell, alias Donald Blue, was a well-kent face and a real character around St Andrews from the 1840s. He was called Donald Blue ever since the day, as a young orphan, he was given a bright blue coat to wear. Donald grew up with the most unlikely splayed feet and was always full of pawky sayings, being an inimitable wit.

Donald was a good golfer, maintaining a scratch handicap for most of his life, who earned his living as a popular caddie whilst living at the tramps' Model Lodging House

in Baker Lane.

He became notoriously well-known for his annual match over the Old Course with a fellow caddie called Stumpie Eye. The game was keenly followed by members of the R. & A. and the match invariably concluded with both men being thrown into the Swilcan Burn.

This photograph of Donald Blue was commissioned by him in 1903 from which he made postcards to advertise his caddying services to visitors to the 'Old'.

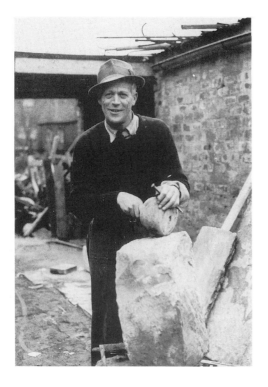

A modern, but rare, character was James K. Wilson ('Just call me J.K.') who returned as a boy to St Andrews in 1914 with his widowed mother. They lived in narrow Market Street and times were hard for the Wilson family. Despite his humble beginnings Jim became a skilled stonemason who worked on many old buildings in the town. For a time he and his wife ran their own business in North Street and Jim gained the reputation of being the best stonemason in the area.

From the 1930s he was well known as a popular off-the-cuff entertainer. He began by playing drums and singing with the local danceband, 'The Harmony Boys', before he began his own one-man show which he played all over Fife as well as organising the 'smokers' at his golf club. He played a mean mandoline, and told jokes and humorous stories both on and off stage.

He was a good golfer, a hobby he took up in middle age with great determination. He beat the legendary Bing Crosby at the British Amateur Open which was held at St Andrews in 1950. After that occasion they became firm friends and often played golf around the country whenever Bing was in Scotland. J.K. was a unique character, someone you couldn't help but take to; so his death, at the age of 81, on Friday 11th March, 1988, came as a blow to a great many in the St Andrews community.

This character was an itinerant organ grinder who visited St Andrews before each Lammas Market from the 1880s. She toured the streets with her birds and monkey, grinding out her music to make what must have been a meagre living. As she wandered around the town with her pony and cart locals would gather round, out of curiosity, or pity, but anyway she was a familiar sight until 1913 when she just stopped coming after over thirty years.

Few communities can lay claim to have had a citizen of the public spirit, versatile gifts and the fearless, if rugged, independence of George Bruce. He began his life as a joiner's apprentice and in time was able to set up his own building business through which he became prosperous. Whilst he worked extremely hard in business, he also wrote and published volumes of poetry; he was a naturalist and he wrote about birds as well as taking leading parts in his own dramatic productions which were held in the, now demolished, fisherfolk quarters in South Castle Street.

He stood as an active and vocal Town Councillor for forty years, working with and fearlessly speaking against the popular Provost Playfair in the mid-1800s. Bruce fought hard for, and worked towards, establishing the natural rights of the downtrodden fishing community and he was the creator of the land extension named after him: The Bruce Embankment which has prevented the sea making inroads into the Old Course.

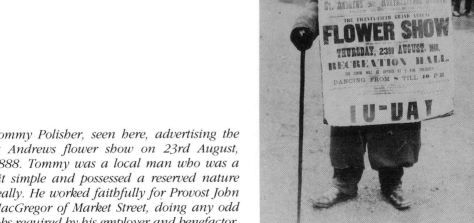

Tommy Polisher, seen here, advertising the St Andrews flower show on 23rd August, 1888. Tommy was a local man who was a bit simple and possessed a reserved nature really. He worked faithfully for Provost John MacGregor of Market Street, doing any odd jobs required by his employer and benefactor.

Andra Kirkaldy was born in March 1860 and as a youngster learned to play golf on the St Andrews Links. He spent more time on the golf course than at school so that he left without being able to read. At the age of 19 he entered the British Open being held at St Andrews. He did well, losing only to the winner on that occasion. After that he left to serve in the Egyptian Campaign and did a tour of duty in India.

He returned to Britain as a civilian and took up the post of golf professional to the Winchester Club, but soon he was back at St Andrews. He was to remain at St Andrews from then on, working as both a professional and a caddie. He was a good golfer, indeed it was said of him that he was the greatest golfer of his time not to have won an Open Championship.

In 1904 he succeeded Tom Morris as honorary professional to the R. & A. Two very different personalities, but both very knowledgeable about the Game. Andra was forthright and blunt of speech — a rough diamond compared to his predecessor — Andra would give freely of his opinions, whether asked or not, as he sat on a high chair positioned between the first tee and the eighteenth hole. He was accurately described as the hairshirt to the self-esteem of the R. & A. members.

Andra had also undertaken caddying (as most professionals did at that time) and did so in his own inimitable way. On one occasion a gentleman golfer had tried in vain to extricate his ball from Hell bunker. He asked his caddie what he should do now. 'If I were ye,' Andra replied, 'A'd tak' th' 9.40 train oot o' St Andraes.'

Old Pat Riley was often seen around the streets of St Andrews during the latter part of last century as he ground the blunted implements of householders. He was quite a character with his easy banter and his great love of his faithful machine.

On one occasion he remarked to a friend that his wife had nearly been run over by a fleeing cart and horse. 'But', he continued, 'she's alright, as you can see', pointing to his old grinding machine. In this photograph Pat is working away in front of the Town Kirk's west door in 1889.

When Sir D'Arcy Wentworth Thompson, C.B., D.Litt., F.R.S., F.R.S.E., Professor of Natural History at the University, died on June 21st, 1948, St Andrews lost one of its most illustrious and unusual citizens. D'Arcy was held in high esteem in the academic world and in affection by townspeople. He was both a humanist and a naturalist concurrently — a rare breed indeed.

D'Arcy arrived in St Andrews in 1917 to take up the University Chair of Natural History. Over the years he contributed with distinction to scholarly modern literature; he was President of the Classical Association, in recognition of his expertise in the ancient language and literature of Greece and Rome. He was also President of the Edinburgh Mathematical Society and the Adviser to the Fishery Board for Scotland. Queen Victoria had made him Commander of the Bath whilst he was further honoured by learned societies and universities throughout Europe.

In St Andrews D'Arcy was known and loved by St Andreans from all walks of life. He was frequently seen walking the town's streets wearing white sandshoes with a live parrot perched on his shoulder. He travelled extensively, and when a colleague once met him on his way to the railway station carrying only a hand-grip the associate greeted him with: 'Hello D'Arcy, off to Edinburgh?' 'No', the scholar replied, 'Off to Delhi.'

D'Arcy himself recalled the late Saturday night when he was travelling on a Dundee tram, when a drunk man spoke to him. 'You are Professor D'Arcy Thompson and you are supposed to be very clever, but I ken something that ye dinna ken. My wife washes yer claes and 'am wearing wan o' yer shirts.' Of his students, D'Arcy once said, 'I don't mind spoon-feeding them, but I draw the line at working their jaws for them.'

This previously unpublished photograph pictures Tom Morris, in his eighty-sixth year in 1907, standing in front of the Home Green and the Royal & Ancient Clubhouse. Tom was born on 16th June, 1821 in North Street and he played golf from the age of six. After being schooled at Madras College he left to work with Allan Robertson making feathery golf balls. He later set up his own ball-manufacturing concern in St Andrews before being employed as a greenkeeper at Prestwick until he was eventually lured back to his native town. Tom then started a small clubmaking business and a retail golf-shop at the Links.

Tom Morris was also a fine golfer who won the Scottish Open on four occasions between 1861 and 1867, thereafter becoming a recognised and much sought-after commentator on the game of golf. Within his own lifetime he was styled 'The Old Man of Golf'. After serving as the R. & A.'s first honorary professional until 1904, he died in May 1908, a legend in his own lifetime and ever since.

The Cinema in St Andrews

ST ANDREANS HAD VIEWED the silent moving films, hand-cranked, from the 1890s in the kinematographic tents at the Lammas Market. However, there were no buildings in St Andrews for putting on film shows until 1909 when the La Scala in James Street was erected. The building was known by locals as the Pamie Ramie and was in fact the former Roman Catholic church which had been situated on the Scores.

Jock Spence's steam traction engine pulls the first third of the former Roman Catholic church (known locally as the 'Tin Tabernacle') from the Scores, through the town's streets and down the steep Melbourne Brae. This photograph was taken by local photographer John Fairweather in 1909 as the engine is about to turn into City Road, past Hope Park Church and the former Alexandra Hotel in St Mary's Place.

Here Jock Spence (pictured on the extreme right) and his men are pictured taking a break during the re-erection of the corrugated-iron and wood structure at James Street, just off Bridge Street, in front of Wallace Street. It was in this building, St Andrews' first picture house, that silent films were shown to local people on a regular basis.

At the beginning of this century the La Scala held regular dances on its beautifully polished wooden floor, community singing, social events and roller skating. Each Sunday evening the La Scala showed silent films in its main hall. Before the audience could watch the films they had to sing a hymn to make the gathering strictly legal and they still had to pay their penny entrance fee.

In 1913 a purpose-built picture house was erected in North Street, between College Street and Muttoes Lane. It was named the Cinema House. At first local people were reluctant to leave the familiar Pamie Ramie, but the superior auditorium and the quality of the pictures on the big screen soon drew in the crowds.

Under the management of Mr Jim Greig the Cinema House showed the latest silent films which were occasionally accompanied by a small orchestra playing incidental music.

(See opposite page)
John Fairweather was commissioned to take this photograph of the Cinema House shortly after it had been equipped to show sound films, or 'talkies', in 1929. Pictured, from the right, are: Jack Humphries, the manager; Jimmy Mitchell, projectionist; Charles Finlay, assistant projectionist; and, on the left, a fifteen-year-old Alex Gourlay who was then the 'winder-boy' and trainee projectionist who remained at the Cinema House for fifty years, becoming the Head Projectionist for many years.

The staff of the New Picture House and their families pose beside the bus that will take them on their holiday outing to Edinburgh in September 1934. The bus is sitting just in front of the pillared canopy at the entrance to the New Picture House in North Street.

The orchestra consisted of Duncan Kirkwood (owner of the City Arms Bar) on piano; Mrs Jessie Kirkwood, violinist; Jim Auchterlonie (plumber) on bass fiddle; Alf Auchterlonie (piano tuner) on drums; Will Stark (clubmaker) on trumpet; and Willie Menzies (baker's van driver) on the clarinet and saxophone. The 'orchestra' played for the big films such as 'Birth of a Nation' on Saturdays and on wet days during the summer tourist season when a large audience was guaranteed. The projectionist and his assistants joined in with the required sound effects by using anything from tin cans and whistles to bells and football rattles. The silent films and the orchestra played at the Cinema House until 1929 when modern projectors and sound-speakers were installed to accommodate the new 'talkies' and the latest 'Movietone' sound-newsreels. Mr Jack Humphries had taken over as the manager the year before when Mr Jim Greig had retired.

A second Cinema building was constructed at the west end of North Street and opened in 1931. It was appropriately named 'The New Picture House' and it gave St Andrews cinemagoers an alternative film venue for the first time. The New Picture House (known

The Golden Anniversary poster which the Cinema House produced for the week of their fiftieth birthday. It was produced by W.C. Henderson on shiny gold paper with royal blue lettering.

Jack Humphries, the Cinema House manager for over fifty years; a Town Councillor who served under six Provosts; a Rotarian and a member of St Andrews Golf Club. He always had a warm welcome for all his customers as he personally supervised the proceedings each evening at the Cinema House. This George Cowie photograph pictures Jack Humphries standing inside the once-familiar auditorium.

and students during the autumn to spring seasons with the bonus of visitors all summer long. All was well, it appeared, until 1st December, 1979 when the local paper devoted its Friday's front page to the story behind the shock headlines:

Manager retires — CINEMA HOUSE IS TO CLOSE

Mr Jack Humphries had been the manager for fifty-one years, since 1928. The Cinema House had opened in 1913 and had given both locals and visitors sixty-six years of film entertainment. The public were given one day's notice that the 'Old' was closing on the Saturday after the evening showing of 'The Buddy Holly Story'; thus a chapter in the modern history of St Andrews ended in an anti-climax.

Being the only Cinema in town now ensures that the New Picture House is well patronised, and the prophets of doom who closed the 'Old' are shown to have failed to anticipate the resurgence of filmgoing among young people and students.

(See opposite page)
The Cinema House was irrevocably closed in December 1979. One feature remains: the stained glass sign seen here. It was rescued, just before demolition, by the District Museum Service who retain it with the intention of having it displayed in the Kinburn House town museum due to open in the early 1990s.

locally as 'The New') boasted that it was 'the home of cosy comfort, courtesy, cleanliness and clear cinematography'. The new building incorporated a large cafeteria, a function suite and a long, tiled foyer with a modern ticket office and a shop where refreshments and snacks were sold. Whilst the queues at the Cinema House (which became 'The Old') had to stand patiently outside, round into Muttoes Lane in all weathers, the foyer of 'The New' could contain and shelter its patrons.

During the week following Monday 2nd December, 1963, the Cinema House celebrated its Golden Jubilee with the screening of Alfred Hitchcock's 'The Birds'. It also showed a rare piece of footage that had been filmed at the beginning of the century in St Andrews. It was billed as post-1918 although it is in fact mostly pre-1918 material showing former buildings, events and characters of the town.

Both the 'Old' and the 'New' carried on showing films to regular audiences of locals

The Cowie Family of Photographers

GEORGE M. COWIE was considered by fellow photographers throughout the Kingdom of Fife and far beyond to be the most exceptional press photographer of his time. He was based in St Andrews from the beginning of the 1930s until his death in 1982, having taken several hundred-thousand photographs around Fife, including a vast number of his adopted town.

Towards the end of his career he donated over 100,000 of his negatives to St Andrews University Library. Years after his death the mammoth task of indexing those negatives, now known as 'The George Cowie

This is a portrait of George Cowie at the age of seventy-nine when he retired after fifty years of photographic work based in St Andrews. He is pictured here with an old bellows tripod camera, which was just one of his personal collection of antique cameras. This photograph was taken by colleague Bill Flett to mark George's retiral from the business in March 1981.

Collection', is only half complete because of the sheer volume of material. George Cowie was a prolific photographer who worked extremely hard in his distinctive style, producing a multitude of pictures, each with exceptional clarity and breadth of vision in the portrayal of an amazing variety of subjects.

In St Andrews alone he covered every noteworthy event including golf championships, coffee mornings, horse parades and degree ceremonies. He captured on film the social and working life of St Andreans, as well as the town's streets and buildings, many of which have either been demolished or altered. He also covered numerous events around Fife — often in collaboration with journalist Alex B. Paterson — including royal visits, parades, highland games, fairs, processions, Fife hunts and boat-launchings; subjects such as Fife farm folk,

Beatrice took this delightful snap of her sisters, Mabel (left) and Maud, with her pet dog, Toby, joining in the fun. In 1919 this photograph gained Beatrice second place in a photo-competition run by the Bulletin, *a pictorial newspaper of the day.*

the East Neuk community and happenings such as car, train and aeroplane crashes.

George Cowie was the front-man of a unique team comprising himself and his wife Beatrice. She faithfully supported him in both his work and life. Beatrice Cowie (née Govan) was already a fully trained professional photographer when George decided to join the firm of which she was a partner. She proved to be a first class portrait photographer and a skilful photographic technician who later took a back seat in order to support George's career by undertaking

George Cowie: the young press photographer who caused quite a stir amongst local chemists, who sold and processed films, when he and his wife set up as Cowie & Govan in the Spring of 1931. Whilst George's entrance to the St Andrews photographic scene was welcomed by the Town Council, it was resented by John Fairweather who had already spent over thirty years as the St Andrews portrait photographer.

This photograph taken by former Provost David Niven, shows the Cowie & Govan shop at 131 South Street. The shop sat between the former G.P.O. wooden telephone kiosks (now a shop frontage) next to the Post Office (right) with Eddie the joiner's close next to Rodger's meal shop (once Haxton the licensed grocer). The Cowie shop boasted a large glass case at the right-hand side of their entrance in which recently taken local photographs were displayed. These were a great attraction to passers-by who could buy their own copies from the Cowies.

This photograph was taken by a street-photographer in December 1943 whilst Alex Paterson was serving as an engineer in the RAF and George in the Royal Engineers. George took volumes of photographs of war damage and scenes at one of the concentration camps in Germany as part of his official Army duties. On this occasion the two friends and colleagues spent a happy time of re-union together, on pass for the day, in Derby which was approximately halfway between their separate bases.

Christmas was always a close family occasion for George and wife Beatrice, seen here in their home at 62 North Street. In their tender moments George would endearingly call his wife by her full Christian name of Beatrice Alice. They only once exhibited their work side by side when each had photographs selected to hang at an international exhibition at Dundee in 1949.

all the processing work, during the early years, matching the exceptional nature of his output and quality.

Their son, Andrew Govan Cowie, was born in May 1937. He grew up in the aura of photography and soon learned the basic techniques of both processing and picture-taking from his parents. His nature was to be more akin to his mother's in preferring a quiet life. In 1955, when he left school to work in the family business he occasionally assisted his father on press assignments, but most of his work lay in the photographic retail shop and in the processing department at their premises in South Street.

Andrew preferred the medium of colour: photographing anything from flowers to animals, the countryside to the town and its environs. He also produced a unique series of local-view calendars which always sold well.

With George often out on assignments his son, Andrew, saw more of his mother and his aunts who stayed for long periods at the Cowies' home. However, George did devote all the time and affection he could to Andrew and this 1940s photograph, with his car in the background, displays the closeness of the family threesome.

In 1957, when Andrew was twenty, he was introduced to the Byre Theatre where he found real friends and an assortment of tasks which he discovered he could do with great enjoyment. He joined the Play Club and assisted both the amateurs and professionals with increasing competence. In time, he became a first-class stage manager and the technician at the Byre, always trying to improve the theatre's facilities. Andrew is pictured here working on the new Byre Theatre lighting system in 1974.

Andrew Cowie died of leukaemia in October 1980. After the funeral his parents realised that they didn't possess a photograph of Andrew before his illness took hold. It's often a fact that photographers are rarely the subject of a camera and it seemed to be so in Andrew's case. However, when Beatrice's sister Mabel mentioned this fact to her son Kenneth he was able to provide what everyone in the family had given up hope of finding. This photo was taken when Kenneth's brother married. Andrew is pictured at the reception in a Dunbar hotel on 23rd July, 1977 when he was forty years of age.

The family of photographers in the fifties, their closeness and shared happiness accurately captured in this photo.

St Andrews Advertisements of 1912

E. WALKER,

STATIONER.

Artists' Materials, Photographs,
Post-Cards, Souvenirs, etc., etc.

Brass and Copper Ware, Leather Goods,
Original Pictures in Oil and Water Colour.

13, Bell Street, St. ANDREWS.

'Phone 56.　　　　'Grams, "Motors, St. Andrews."

ANDREW A. DUNCAN & SONS,
MOTOR AGENTS and Repairers.

FIRST-CLASS CARS FOR HIRE.
Official Repairers to Lloyd's.
Largely extended premises. New Garage of model
design, embodying the best features.
LADIES' ROOM.　　　CHAUFFEURS' ROOM.
Eight Private Lock-up Compartments.
OFFICIAL AGENTS TO "A.A. & M.U."

2, ST. MARY'S PLACE, **ST. ANDREWS.**
52, ARGYLE STREET,

JAMES PIRIE,

*China, Glass and
Earthenware Merchant,*

131, SOUTH STREET,

(Opposite ——
ROYAL HOTEL.) ST. ANDREWS.

BREAKFAST	TEA	
DINNER } SETS.	TRINKET } SETS.	
DESSERT	BEDROOM	

VASES of every description in China and Glass
for Table Decoration.

Sole Agent in St. Andrews for
**WEMYSS WARE, WEDGWOOD HERALDIC
WARE and ROYAL ARITA PORCELAIN.**
CHINA neatly repaired.

Telephone No. 15.

Established over
70 Years.

A. & L. HENDRY.

BUTCHERS,
POULTERERS
and GAME DEALERS

(Opposite Post Office, to the East),

104, South St., ST. ANDREWS.

Only the Choicest Qualities in Home-fed Beef,
Mutton, Lamb and Veal. Salted Rounds, Corned
Beef and Pickled Tongues. Every Variety in the
Trade Supplied.
HIGHEST QUALITY. LOWEST PRICES.
Finest Pressed Beef always ready—a speciality.
The " St. Andrews " Scotch Haggis, made by
ourselves, is a perfect treat.
*ORDERS CALLED FOR every morning and delivered with
the greatest promptitude.*
— A TRIAL SOLICITED —

C. B. MACFARLANE

Grocer and House Agent.

Up-to-date list of

— FURNISHED HOUSES AND APARTMENTS —

with Plan and Guide free. Kindly state requirements.

ST. ANDREWS.

JAS. A. DUFF,

"Central" Hairdressing Saloon,

103, MARKET STREET,
(Near the Fountain,)

:: ST. ANDREWS. ::

Agent for Mois Clansman and Keystone Razors.

ANTISEPTICS ALWAYS IN USE.

LARGE SELECTIONS OF
RAZORS, : STROPS,
BRUSHES, : COMBS
AND HAIR NETS
ALWAYS IN STOCK.

Razors Ground and Set.

:: :: A BRIGHT, AIRY SALOON. :: ::

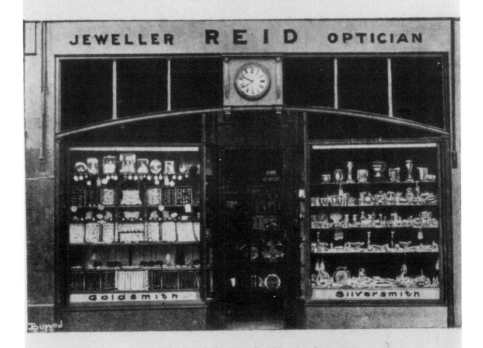

DISPENSING and PHOTOGRAPHIC CHEMISTS.

SMITH & GOVAN,

Plates, Films, Paper, Developer and all
Photographic Requisites.

Amateurs' Negatives Developed and Printed.

MAKERS AND PROPRIETORS OF THE
Original "St. Andrews Curry Powder."
New Dentifrice "Borodonto" (Regtd.)
Famous *Genuine* "*Old* Lavender Water." &c., &c.

109, SOUTH STREET,

ST. ANDREWS.

Established 1822.   'Phone: No. 6.